INTRODUCTION
...and why I decided to write this book.

Dear readers;

Bnei Brak, my birth city, stands apart from all other cities in Eretz Yisrael. It possesses a unique character and beauty all its own. Unlike many other cities and settlements in Israel, Bnei Brak was built by *frum* Yidden with the express goal of creating a Torah-true place where Yidden will learn Torah and proudly observe all the mitzvos.

Fulfilling this dream was not easy, but they persevered, and with a lot of *siyata diShmaya*, today the city is filled with Torah institutions and beautiful *frum*, Yiddishe families. At some point, the city rightfully earned the title "City of Torah and *chassidus*."

It is hard to imagine, but the densely-populated city teeming with people and cars that we know today was once just a haphazard group of huts erected by a handful of devoted Chassidim on desolate desert land. Already as a child, I heard and read extensively about those days, about the modest houses that were constructed to replace the huts (one of which my own grandmother, a"h, lived in), the fruit trees lovingly planted by the settlers, and the special sense of community that the founding families shared.

I was always captivated by the image of the jackals roaming the desert, their howls piercing the night, mingling with the hoots of the owls. Today, these sounds of nature have been replaced by the honking of cars and the clamor of humanity filling every available space. The dark dirt roads have made way to tall, overcrowded buildings completely obscuring the horizon. Still, Bnei Brak remains a city of beauty for those who sense its depths and realize just how completely and amazingly the early settlers' dreams have been fulfilled.

And that is why I decided to write this book about Bnei Brak's early years. While the story is completely fictional, it is intricately woven with authentic historical facts and recreates the unique atmosphere of those early days.

I'd like to thank *Marveh Latzame*, the weekly family magazine, for hosting my comic story within its pages. I'd like to thank my readers – especially those who took the time to write to me and express how much they were enjoying the story. Thank you to my precious children, who helped me build the characters, most notably Mottele and Baruchke, and lead them through the twists and turns of the plot.

In writing this book, I culled valuable historic information from the books *Al Chomotayich Bnei Brak* by Rabbi Yitzchak Meir, z"l, and *Chevlei Yotzer* by, yblc"t, Rabbi Aharon Sorasky *shlita*.

E. Eichler

Translated, Edited & Typeset by:
Deena Weinberg

Distributed by:

Lechaim Productions Inc.
Tel: 718-369-2090, Fax: 718-369-2092
1529 Dean Street, Brooklyn NY 11213
info@lchaimusa.com
www.lchaimusa.com

All rights reserved.
Lechaim Productions Inc.
No part of this book may be reproduced in any form, by any means, mechanical or electronic, including photocopy, translation and recording, without written permission from the publisher.

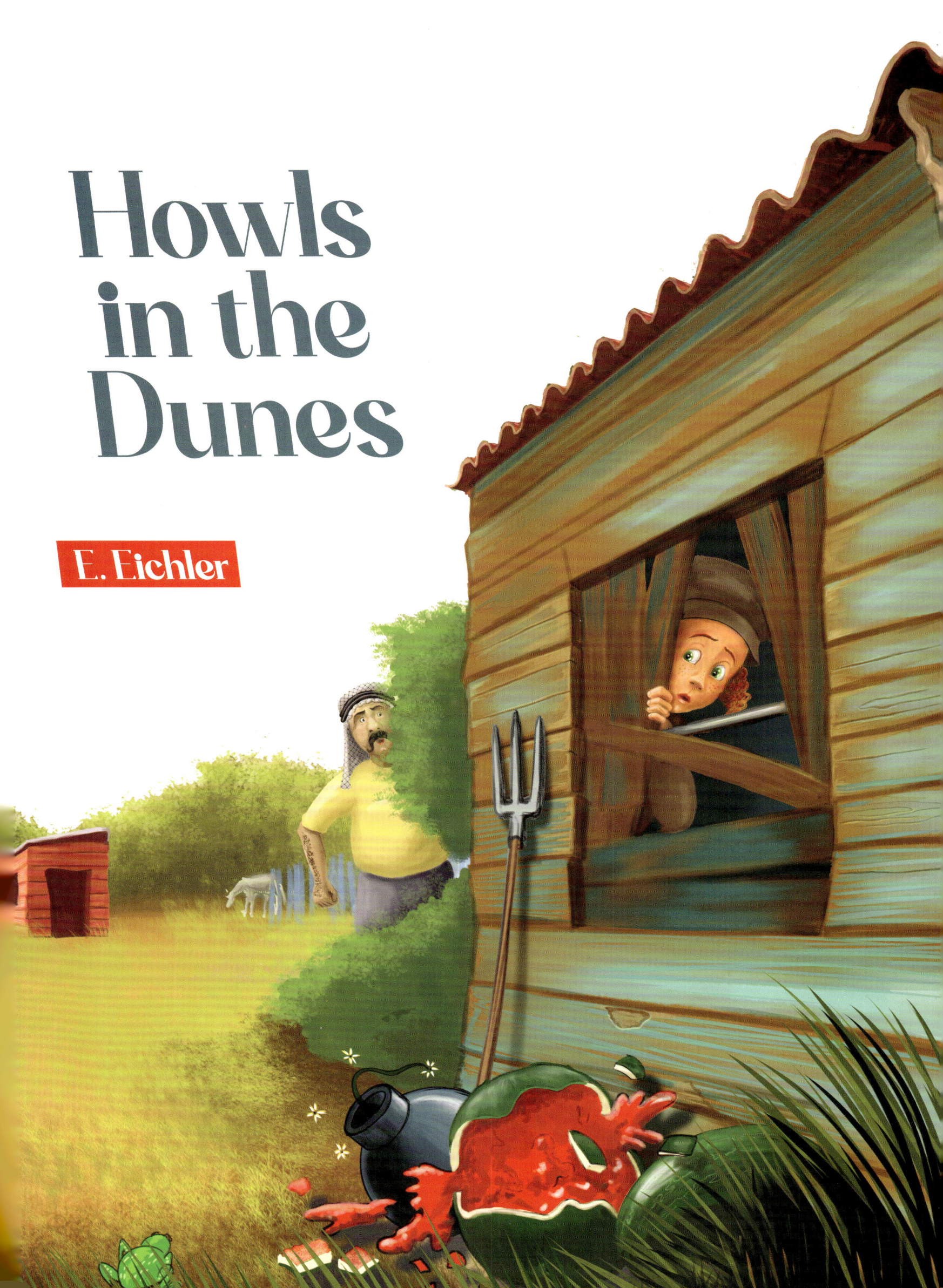

* KINDERLACH – CHILDREN

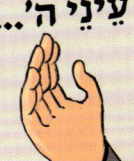

* KESUBOS 111A

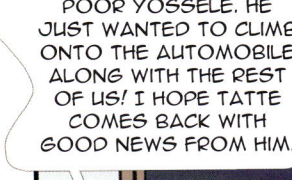

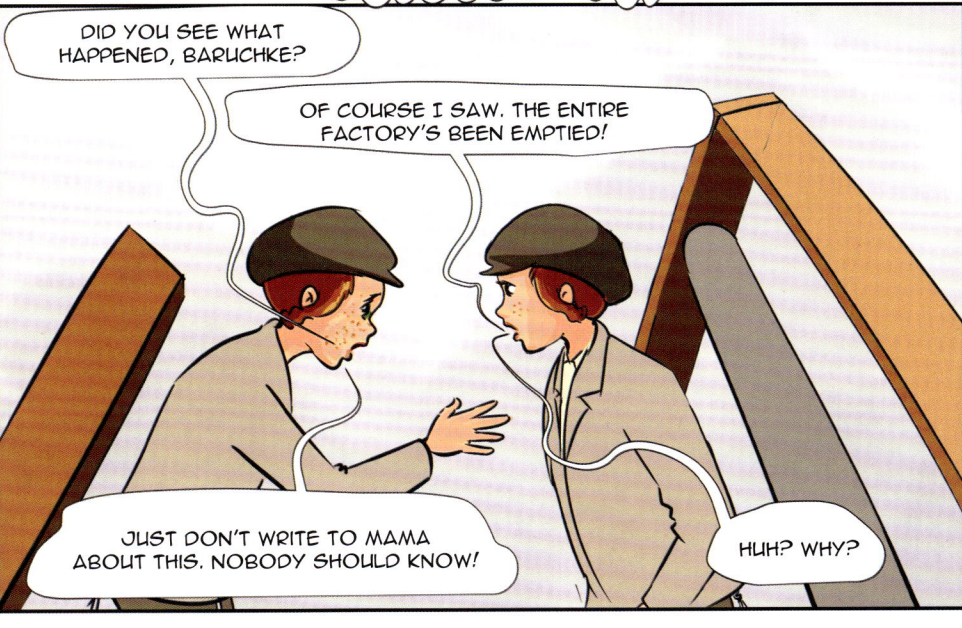

HERE, MOTTELE. SPREAD THESE WHITE TABLECLOTHS ON THE TABLES FOR SHABBOS. I'LL SWEEP THE FLOOR.
WELL, MOTTELE? WHAT DO YOU SAY ABOUT OUR NEW CITY? ARE YOU SETTLING IN?
LEKAVOD SHABBOS KODESH!
YES, TATTE. BUT I REALLY MISS MAMA AND LITTLE ESTHER!
I UNDERSTAND. I HOPE THAT VERY SOON THEY'LL BE ABLE TO JOIN US HERE. MAMA MISSES YOU BOTH SO MUCH TOO.
ARE YOU MAKING FRIENDS HERE?
YES. I REALLY LIKE THE BOYS.
WHAT ABOUT BARUCHKE?
BARUCHKE IS HAVING A HARD TIME...
PLEASE TRY TO HELP HIM, MOTTELE. HE'S NOT AS SOCIAL AS YOU ARE. YOU CAN HELP HIM MAKE FRIENDS!
MOST IMPORTANTLY, YOU SHOULD BE HIS FRIEND. FOR SOME REASON YOU FIGHT A LOT. TRY TO SEE WHERE YOU CAN BE NICER TO HIM. YOU'LL NEVER LOSE OUT FROM BEING NICE.
WHAT HAPPENED TO ABDUL? WHY'S HE SO UPSET?
HE'S UPSET THAT I SPOKE TO HIS SON ABOUT THE FABRICS.
I WON'T TELL THEM ABOUT MY SUSPICIONS. THEY MIGHT MAKE FUN OF ME.
I DON'T LIKE THAT KID. HE'S TOO CUNNING. WE'D BETTER MAKE SURE HE DOESN'T COME BACK HERE. D'YOU HEAR, MOHAMMAD?
BUT HE ALWAYS COMES HERE TO BUY WATERMELONS. ISN'T THAT GOOD FOR US?
NO! HE'S DANGEROUS. I DON'T WANT THE POLICE COMING HERE. UNDERSTOOD?! DON'T YOU EVER TALK TO HIM AGAIN – NOT ABOUT FABRICS, AND NOT ABOUT ANYTHING ELSE!

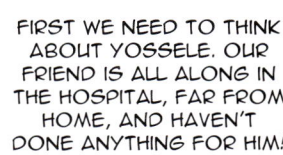

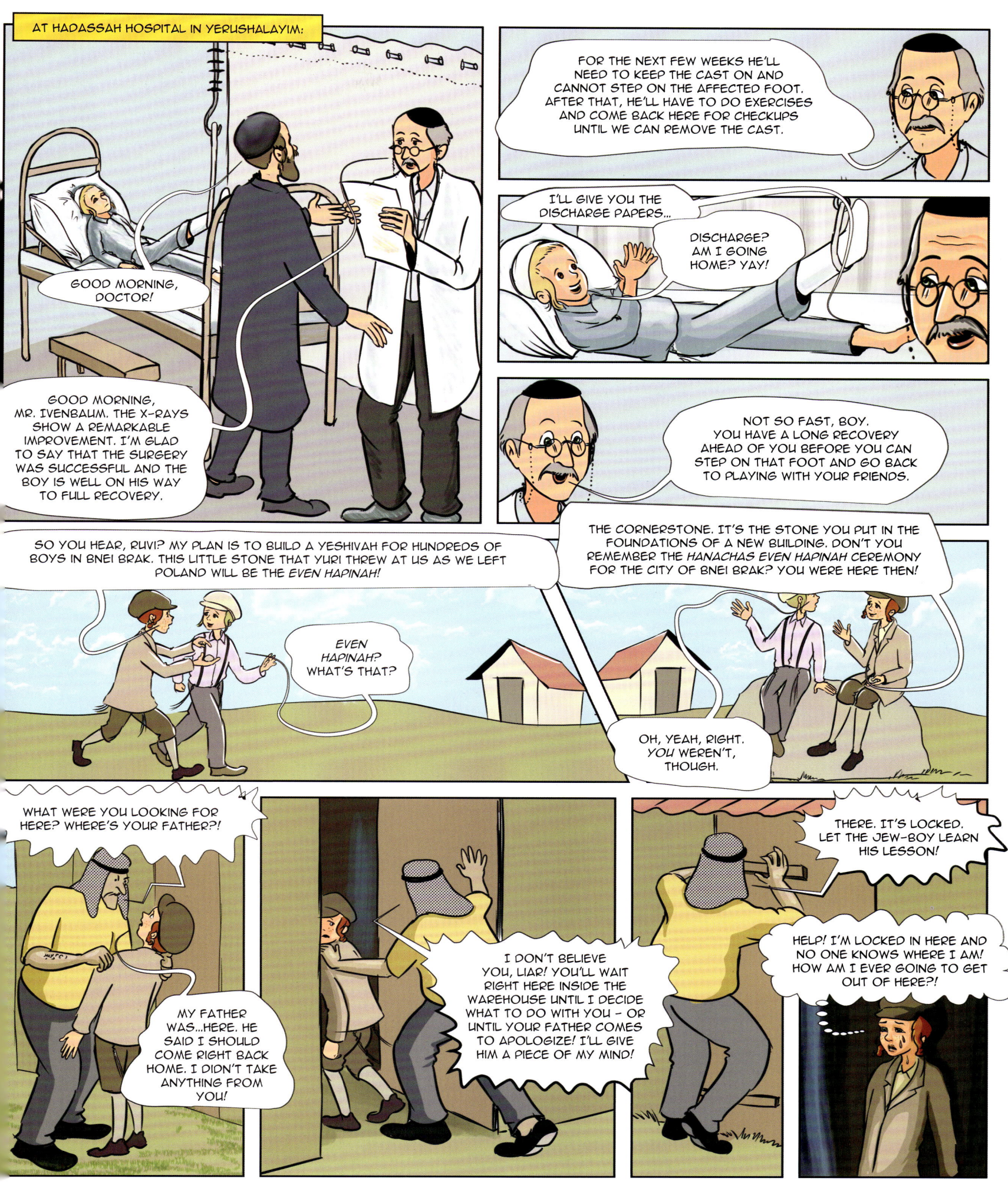

HALIL, MOHAMMAD, LISTEN TO WHAT YOUR FATHER'S GOING TO TELL YOU. YOU KNOW THOSE *YAHUD* WHO SETTLED NEAR OUR VILLAGE? WE MUST SCARE THEM AWAY FROM HERE.
WHY? THEY'RE GOOD FOR BUSINESS.
DIDN'T YOU YOURSELF SAY THAT ONLY A FEW DAYS AGO?
YOU WANT TO SEE WHY? I'LL TELL YOU WHY!
INSIDE ABDUL'S WAREHOUSE:
MY EYES HAVE GOTTEN USED TO THE DARK AND I CAN FINALLY SEE AROUND ME.
I'LL TRY TO LOOK FOR SOME KIND OF SHARP OBJECT TO BREAK THE DOOR.
SEE THAT HILL OVER THERE, RUVI? THAT'S WHERE I WANT TO BUILD THE YESHIVAH. THE HILL OVERLOOKS THE ENTIRE SETTLEMENT. IT WILL BE LIKE THE CITY'S LIGHTHOUSE!
WOW, MOTTELE. YOU KNOW A LOT OF FANCY WORDS!
YOU MEAN "LIGHTHOUSE"? I SAW ONE WHEN WE ARRIVED HERE ON THE SHIP. THAT'S WHEN I THOUGHT OF THE IDEA.
SOMEHOW YOU ALWAYS SEE ALL THE INTERESTING THINGS.
I EVEN DREW IT IN MY NOTEBOOK. AND THEN I THOUGHT THAT IT'S A FITTING DESCRIPTION FOR THE YESHIVAH, WHICH WILL LIGHT UP THE ENTIRE CITY WITH ITS TORAH LEARNING! WANT TO SEE THE DRAWING?

IN THE SHUL IN BNEI BRAK, MINCHAH DAVENING DRAWS TO A CLOSE:
WHY ISN'T BARUCHKE HERE YET? FIXING HIS SHOE SHOULDN'T HAVE TAKEN MORE THAN 5-10 MINUTES!
AFTER MINCHAH THERE'S A DAF YOMI SHIUR, AND THEN MAARIV. I HOPE I'LL SEE HIM HERE BY MAARIV.
I'M A LITTLE WORRIED... IS HE FAMILIAR ENOUGH WITH THE WAY BACK?
SEE THIS HAND GRENADE? I SAVED IT FROM A JEW-BOY'S HANDS JUST BEFORE HE TOOK IT FOR HIMSELF.
LEMONADE? HUH? THAT DOES NOT LOOK ANYTHING LIKE LEMONADE. IT'S BLACK!
WOAH, SCARY.
NOT LEMONADE! IT'S A BOMB! IT CAN KILL FIVE PEOPLE IN ONE GO!
HOW DID THE KID GET HIS HANDS ON IT?
HE FOUND IT BURIED IN THE EARTH NEAR THE WATERMELON PATCH.
HERE YOU CAN SEE US ON THE SHIP, LOOKING AHEAD AT THE LIGHTHOUSE LIGHTING UP THE PORT.
AND THIS IS THE YESHIVAH THAT I WANT TO BUILD. IT'S LIKE A SPIRITUAL LIGHTHOUSE!
LET'S RUN TO SHUL FOR MAARIV NOW. MY FATHER MUST BE WAITING FOR ME THERE ALREADY.

HELLO, MOTTELE. HAVE YOU SEEN BARUCHKE ANYWHERE? IS HE AT HOME?

I'M NOT COMING FROM HOME NOW, TATTE. I WAS OUTSIDE WITH RUVI UNTIL NOW.

I'LL RUN HOME TO SEE IF BARUCHKE'S THERE. IT'S DARK OUTSIDE AND I WANT TO MAKE SURE HE ARRIVED HOME SAFELY.

HOW DID I GET MYSELF INTO THIS MESS?! TATTE WAS SO SURE THAT I'LL FOLLOW HIM FIVE MINUTES LATER, AND INSTEAD I'M STUCK HERE WITH NO WAY TO ESCAPE!

I WISH MOTTELE WAS HERE. HE WOULD HAVE FOUND SOME KIND OF SOLUTION.

HE ALWAYS HAS GREAT IDEAS TO SOLVE ANY PROBLEM. I WISH HE WAS HERE WITH ME. LATELY WE'VE BECOME SO DISTANCED, AND NOW I SEE HOW SAD THAT IS.

HASHEM, I PROMISE YOU THAT IF YOU SOMEHOW GET ME OUT OF HERE, I'LL ALWAYS MAKE SURE TO GET ALONG WITH MY BROTHER. I'LL NEVER, EVER FIGHT WITH HIM ANYMORE!

AT LEAST THERE'S ONE BENEFIT TO MY STAY HERE IN THE HOSPITAL. I PICKED UP SOME ARABIC! WHO KNOWS, IT MIGHT PROVE TO BE USEFUL SOMEDAY.

IN THE HOSPITAL:

ALI, HALAYOM HALVALAD BAHIMSHI MINHON, BADAL ALVA'I.*

AH? BAHIMSHI MINHON?

* "ALI, THE BOY'S LEAVING HERE TODAY. CHANGE THE SHEETS."
** "LEAVING?"

41

42

IN BNEI BRAK:
THAT'S A GOOD IDEA. MOTTELE, GO WITH REB TZVI. YUSUF WILL SEE YOU AND UNDERSTAND WHOM WE'RE LOOKING FOR.
ALL THE MEN IN THE VILLAGE JOIN THE SEARCH EFFORTS, LOOKING EVERYWHERE USING LANTERNS, OIL LAMPS, MATCHES, TORCHES ANY ANYTHING THAT CAN LIGHT UP THE DARKNESS.
ALL THE LIGHTS ARE OUT ALREADY IN THE ARAB VILLAGE. MOST OF THE VILLAGERS GO TO SLEEP EARLY AND WAKE UP WITH THE ROOSTERS.
WHERE CAN BARUCHKE BE?! OH! THERE'S YUSUF'S SHED. IT SEEMS TO BE EMPTY AND LOCKED UP.
HEY, WHAT ARE THOSE SOUNDS?
IN ABDUL'S WAREHOUSE:
BARUCHKE FALLS ASLEEP, EXHAUSTED FROM THE DAY'S EVENTS.
YOSSELE AND HIS FATHER RETURN TO BNEI BRAK:
OUCH! OOOWW! VERY BUMP ON THE OAD HURTS MY FOOT SO BADLY!
EXCUSE ME, DRIVER, CAN YOU TRY TO DRIVE A BIT MORE SLOWLY? MY SON IS RECOVERING FROM SURGERY AND THE DRIVE IS DIFFICULT FOR HIM.
YOSSELE, PLACE YOUR FOOT ON MY KNEES. I HOPE THAT WILL MAKE IT EASIER FOR YOU. LOOK, WE'RE ALMOST IN RAMAT GAN ALREADY.
BUT FROM RAMAT GAN WE STILL NEED TO GET TO BNEI BRAK, AND THINGS WILL ONLY GET WORSE! THERE'S NO PAVED ROAD, ONLY BUMPY HILLS AND HOWLING WILD DOGS...
אִם אָמַרְתִּי מָטָה רַגְלִי, מָטָה רַגְלִי...
חַסְדְּךָ... יִסְעָדֵנִי...

I'D BETTER GIVE THAT JEW-BOY SOMETHING TO EAT. TOMORROW I'LL SEND HIM HOME. HE'LL HAVE LEARNED HIS LESSON!
AAAAAAAAH, I'M SO TIRED!
WHAT'S THAT SOUND? VISITORS TO THE VILLAGE? AT THIS HOUR?!
AM I DREAMING? IT'S... IT'S THE JEW-BOY I LOCKED UP IN MY WAREHOUSE - ON THAT HORSE! HOW'S HE MANAGE TO ESACPE?!
IF THEY ACCUSE ME OF KIDNAPPING THE BOY, I'M IN BIG TROUBLE. WHAT SHOULD I DO?!
!!
THAT MAN HAS A GUN! HE'S COMING HERE TO TAKE REVENGE! I'D BETTER FIND A PLACE TO HIDE.
THERE'S NO SIGN OF A JEWISH BOY ANYWHERE HERE. MOTTELE, LET'S DAVEN TO HASHEM NOW. IT'S THE BEST WE CAN DO FOR BARUCHKE!
BARUCHKE! BARUCHKE!
USKUT*!
INSIDE THE WAREHOUSE:
BARUCHKE SLEEPS DEEPLY, COVERING HIMSELF IN FABRICS STOLEN FROM HIS FATHER'S FACTORY TO WARM HIMSELF.
I DON'T THINK WE HAVE ANOTHER CHOICE. WE'LL GO HOME ANOW AND RETURN AFTER DAWN. THE VILLAGERS ARE ALL FAST ASLEEP.
HASHEM, PLEASE PROTECT MY BROTHER BARUCHKE. I'M NEVER GOING TO FIGHT WITH HIM ANYMORE!

* QUIET!

BNEI BRAK!
I ALMOST FORGOT WHAT THE SETTLEMENT LOOKS LIKE. I'VE BEEN AWAY FOR SO LONG!
WHAT'S EVERYONE DOING OUTSIDE AT THIS HOUR? THEY LOOK LIKE A WELCOMING COMMITTEE, COMING TO GREET US WITH TORCHES AND LAMPS!
I HEAR A CAR APPROACHING. SOMEONE'S COMING! MAYBE THEY FOUND BARUCHKE!
OH, IT'S MR. IVENBAUM. YOSSELE'S BACK! HOW WONDERFUL!
OY, HE STILL CAN'T WALK!
THIS IS SO EMBARRASSING! EVERYONE'S WATCHING TATTE PICKING ME UP LIKE A BABY.
SHALOM ALEICHEM, REB IVENBAUM! I SEE YOSSELE'S BACK HOME, BARUCH HASHEM! IS THERE ANYTHING WE CAN DO TO HELP?
BARUCH HASHEM.
WHAT'S GOING ON HERE? WHY'S EVERYONE OUTSIDE IN MIDDLE OF THE NIGHT?
WE'RE LOOKING FOR A MISSING CHILD.
A MISSING CHILD?! WHO?!
BARUCHKE YISRAELOVICH.
GASP... *GASP*... WHERE SHOULD I GO? I KNOW! THE WATERMELON PATCH. I'LL LIE AMONG THE WATERMELONS AND NO ONE WILL SEE ME.

Panel 1: AHHHH. GOOD MORNING, WATERMELONS! WHAT WAS IT LIKE TO HAVE A MIDNIGHT VISITOR?

Panel 2: JAMILA! WHERE'S MY COFF... WHOOPS, I FORGOT. JAMILA CAN'T HEAR ME.

Panel 3: BUT HOW AM I GOING TO MANAGE WITHOUT MY COFFEE?!

Panel 4: ABI*! WE WERE LOOKING FOR YOU! HOW DID YOU GET HERE?

Panel 5: OH, HALIL AND MOHAMMAD! HOW'D YOU KNOW TO COME HERE? I URGENTLY NEED YOUR HELP.

Panel 6: YOSSELE, WE MISSED YOU SO MUCH! WE'RE GOING TO TAKE YOU OUT ON A LITTLE OUTING BEFORE *CHEDER* STARTS.

NEARBY, IN BNEI BRAK:

Panel 7: I MISS SEEING THE GROVES OUTSIDE THE SETTLEMENT. CAN YOU TAKE ME THERE?

Panel 8: WE'D BETTER HURRY, THOUGH. RAV FRIEDMAN DOESN'T LIKE IT WHEN WE'RE LATE TO *CHEDER*.

LET'S KEEP OUR EYES OPEN. WE MIGHT EVEN FIND BARUCHKE SOMEWHERE!

INSIDE THE WAREHOUSE IN IBN IBRAQ:

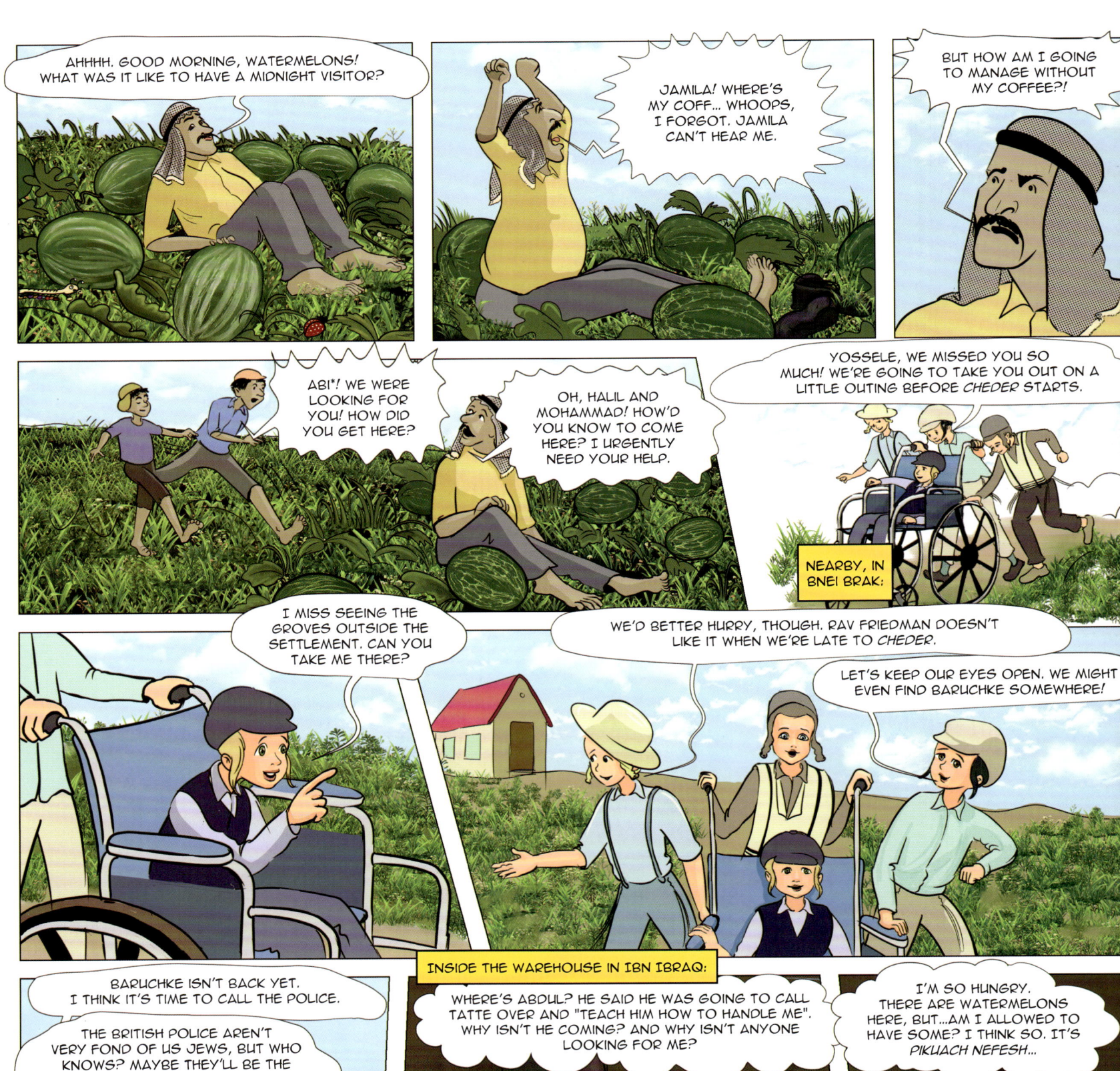

Panel 9: BARUCHKE ISN'T BACK YET. I THINK IT'S TIME TO CALL THE POLICE.

THE BRITISH POLICE AREN'T VERY FOND OF US JEWS, BUT WHO KNOWS? MAYBE THEY'LL BE THE ONES TO FIND BARUCHKE.

Panel 10: WHERE'S ABDUL? HE SAID HE WAS GOING TO CALL TATTE OVER AND "TEACH HIM HOW TO HANDLE ME". WHY ISN'T HE COMING? AND WHY ISN'T ANYONE LOOKING FOR ME?

Panel 11: I'M SO HUNGRY. THERE ARE WATERMELONS HERE, BUT...AM I ALLOWED TO HAVE SOME? I THINK SO. IT'S *PIKUACH NEFESH*...

* FATHER

Panel 1:
- WHY DID YOU SLEEP IN THE WATERMELON PATCH, ABI?
- WHY'RE YOU ASKING DUMB QUESTIONS?!

Panel 2:
- ABI, UMI* WAS VERY NERVOUS WHEN SHE SAW YOU WEREN'T HOME!

Panel 3:
- I'LL TELL YOU WHAT HAPPENED. LAST NIGHT I CAUGHT A YOUNG YAHUD SNOOPING AROUND OUR WAREHOUSE. YOU KNOW, THE WAREHOUSE FILLED WITH FABRICS THAT WE STOLE FROM BNEI BRAK.

Panel 4:
- WHAT AMAZING HASHGACHAH! HASHEM LED US HERE JUST IN TIME!
- CAN YOU BELIEVE IT?! I TOOK THAT JEW-BOY AND LOCKED HIM UP INSIDE THE WAREHOUSE TO TEACH HIM A LESSON. SERVES HIM RIGHT! I MEANT TO LET HIM OUT LATER AND TELL HIS FATHER A THING OR TWO ABOUT HOW TO RAISE KIDS, BUT THEN IN MIDDLE OF THE NIGHT, I SAW THE BOY WALKING AROUND OUTSIDE! I HAVE NO IDEA HOW HE LET HIMSELF OUT. HE WAS RIDING ON A HORSE BEHIND A JEW HOLDING A GUN.

Panel 5:
- I'LL BET THEY WERE SEARCHING FOR ME TO ACCUSE ME OF KIDNAPPING.

Panel 6:
- THEY MIGHT EVEN BE PLANNING TO HAND ME OVER TO THE POLICE!

Panel 7:
- OBVIOUSLY, I DIDN'T WANT THEM TO FIND ME, SO I HID HERE IN THE PATCH.

Panel 8:
- THAT'S STRANGE. WE DIDN'T HEAR ANYTHING. HOW DID THE BOY MANAGE TO BREAK OUT OF THE WAREHOUSE WITHOUT MAKING A SOUND?
- I DON'T KNOW. WHATEVER. DIDN'T YOU BRING ME ANYTHING TO EAT?!

Panel 9:
- HEY! SOMEONE'S HIDING BEHIND THOSE BUSHES!

* MOTHER

RUN!
WHY? WE DIDN'T DO ANYTHING WRONG. WE'RE ALLOWED TO BE HERE!
WE CAN'T RUN VERY FAST WITH THE WHEELCHAIR ANYWAY.
LEAVE THE WHEELCHAIR HERE. I'LL TRY TO WALK.
WHAT ARE YOU TALKING ABOUT?! NO!!
SO WHAT SHOULD WE DO?!
YOU! WHAT ARE YOU DOING HERE?!
THOSE *YAHUD'S* KIDS AGAIN! ALWAYS STICKING THEIR NOSES IN OTHER PEOPLE'S BUSINESS!
WE'RE JUST WALKING AROUND. WHY DO YOU CARE?
I'LL THROW THIS WATERMELON ON THEIR HEADS. IT'S HEAVY!
BOOM! SPLAT!
MEANWHILE, IN ABDUL'S WAREHOUSE:
HASHEM, THANK YOU FOR THE WATERMELONS. IT WAS A BIT HARD TO CRACK THEM OPEN, BUT THEY'RE DELICIOUS!
BARUCH ATAH... BOREI PRI HA'ADAMAH!

WHEW! WHAT A *NESS!* THE WATERMELON COULD'VE HIT OUR HEADS!
LEAVE THEM ALONE. I DON'T KNOW WHAT CAME OVER ME. ONE NIGHT IN THE PATCH AND I'VE TURNED INTO A WATERMELON MYSELF.
THOSE KIDS CAN'T DO ANYTHING TO US. THEY DID NOT UNDERSTAND WHAT WE WERE SAYING. WE WERE SPEAKING ARABIC!
IF NO ONE'S COME TO OUR HOUSE UNTIL NOW, AND THE POLICE ISN'T EXACTLY KNOWN TO HELP THE JEWS, THE BOY MUST HAVE BEEN TOO AFRAID TO TELL ANYONE WHAT HE SAW IN THE WAREHOUSE. OR MAYBE HE DIDN'T EVEN SEE IT IN THE DARK.
I'LL MOVE THE FABRICS TO A SAFER PLACE. BUT FOR NOW, THE MOST URGENT MATTER TO ATTEND TO IS BREAKFAST. I'M STARVING!
WE'RE RUNNING QUICKLY AND THE WHEELCHAIR KEEPS BOUNCING. I HOPE WE'RE NOT HURTING YOU, YOSSELE.
NEVER MIND. LET'S JUST GET BACK TO THE SETTLEMENT AS QUICKLY AS POSSIBLE. I MUST TELL TATTE WHAT I HEARD. ABDUL KNOWS WHERE BARUCHKE IS!
FASTER! FASTER! POOR BARUCHKE, LOCKED UP INSIDE ABDUL'S WAREHOUSE SINCE LAST NIGHT!
EVERYONE'S IN SHUL NOW. LET'S GO THERE.
I'M HEADING OUT TO TEL AVIV NOW TO GET THE POLICE INVOLVED. YOU KEEP DAVENING AND SEARCHING.

LET'S HEAD BACK TO IBN IBRAQ TO CONTINUE OUR SEARCH.
ME TOO?
MOTTELE, YOU STAY HERE TODAY. YOUR TORAH LEARNING WILL BE A LOT MORE HELPFUL FOR OUR SEARCH.
REB YISRAELOVICH! YOSSELE HAS SOMETHING VERY IMPORTANT TO TELL YOU!
NOT NOW, KIDS. DON'T YOU SEE HOW BUSY REB YISRAELOVICH IS? WE'RE LOOKING FOR BARUCHKE. NOTHING ELSE MATTERS NOW.
IT HAS TO DO WITH BARUCHKE'S DISAPPEARANCE!
WE WERE OUT IN THE FIELDS, AND WE OVERHEARD ABDUL TALKING TO HIS SONS IN THE WATERMELON PATCH.
SO EARLY IN THE MORNING?
ABDUL SLEPT IN THE PATCH! HIS SONS CAME THERE LOOKING FOR HIM, AND HE TOLD THEM THAT HE SLEPT THERE BECAUSE HE WAS HIDING FROM THE *YAHUD*, WHO WILL PROBABLY WANT TO TAKE REVENGE OF HIM BECAUSE HE LOCKED A JEWISH BOY INSIDE HIS WAREHOUSE!
THESE KIDS HAVE SOME IMAGINATION.
THAT JUST DOESN'T MAKE ANY SENSE. ABDUL IS OUR FRIEND. ANYWAY, THEY MUST'VE SPOKEN ARABIC. HOW COULD YOU HAVE UNDERSTOOD WHAT THEY WERE SAYING?!

WE'RE HEADING BACK TO IBN IBRAQ NOW TO MEET YUSUF, THE SHOEMAKER. WE'LL ALSO TRY TO SEE IF WE CAN FIND ABDUL'S WAREHOUSE.
THEY DIDN'T TAKE US SERIOUSLY. I WISH THEY WOULD! I'M SURE ABDUL KNOWS WHERE BARUCHKE IS!
WE'D BETTER HEAD TO THE *CHEDER* NOW. IT'S LATE!
HEY, BOYS! WE'RE STARTING TO DAVEN NOW. HURRY UP!
I'M GOING TO TELL MY FATHER. I'M SURE HE'LL BELIEVE ME.
OH, YOSSELE! YOU'RE JOINING US TODAY! HOW NICE!
WELCOME BACK!
THERE'S SOMETHING I MUST TELL MY FATHER. IT'S URGENT!
REB TZVI, WHY DON'T WE PASS THROUGH THE WATERMELON PATCH AND SEE WHETHER ABDUL IS REALLY THERE?
NO PROBLEM. IT'S NOT TOO MUCH OUT OF OUR WAY, AND IT WILL MAKE THE KIDS FEEL GOOD TO KNOW THAT WE TRIED.
THERE'S NO ONE HERE. THE FIELD IS COMPLETELY EMPTY, SAVE FOR ABDUL'S WATERMELONS.
YEAH, I FIGURED SO. KIDS' IMAGINATIONS CAN RUN PRETTY WILD SOMETIMES.
GIDDYAP, HORSE! TO IBN IBRAQ, AS FAST AS YOU CAN!

INSIDE THE WAREHOUSE:

I DAVENED SHACHARIS, I ATE A WATERMELON, AND I'M DEFINITELY FEELING BETTER NOW. I THINK I'LL TRY TO BREAK OFF SOME OF THE BOARDS NAILED TO THE WINDOW.

CRACK! CRAAAACK!

OY, IT'S MAKING A RACKET!

THERE! THIS PIECE OF METAL FROM TATTE'S LOOP WILL BE HELPFUL. THANK YOU, HASHEM, FOR GIVING ME THE IDEA TO LOOK FOR IT!

I DON'T WANT ABDUL TO COME LOOKING FOR THE SOURCE OF THE NOISE. I'D BETTER WAIT UNTIL NIGHTTIME TO CONTINUE.

...BUT IF I WAIT FOR NIGHTTIME, THE SOUNDS WILL BE EVEN MORE AUDIBLE.

MEANWHILE, IN BNEI BRAK:

PIKUACH NEFESH? WHY DON'T YOU TELL ME WHAT THIS IS ABOUT. MAYBE I CAN HELP.

MY FRIENDS TOOK ME TO ABDUL'S WATERMELON PATCH, AND WE OVERHEARD HIM TELLING HIS SONS, WHO HAD COME SEARCHING FOR HIM, THAT HE SLEPT IN THE PATCH BECAUSE HE WAS HIDING FROM THE *YAHUD*. HE SAID WE WERE GOING TO BE UPSET AT HIM FOR HIDING A JEWISH BOY IN HIS WAREHOUSE!

I HEAR. BUT REB YISRAELOVICH ALREADY WENT OUT WITH REB TZVI TO IBN IBRAQ. IT'S BEING TAKEN CARE OF. THERE'S NO POINT IN RUNNING TO YOUR FATHER TOO NOW. DON'T WORRY, YOSSELE.

IN IBN IBRAQ:

AAAAH. I WAS STARVING! MAHMUD, WHERE'S HALIL? START PACKING UP THE FABRICS AND LOAD THEM ONTO THE WAGON!

HALIL! HALIL!!! WHAT ARE YOU DOING OVER THERE?!

52

WHAT ARE YOU DOING OVER THERE?
I JUST WANT TO SEE HOW THIS...
BOOM!
INSIDE THE WAREHOUSE:
WOAH, WHAT WAS THAT?!
WE'VE REACHED THE ARAB VILLAGE. DO YOU SMELL SMOKE TOO?
THE ARABS BURN THEIR GARBAGE. OR MAYBE THEY'RE HOLDING A BARBEQUE OR SOMETHING.
NO, REB TZVI. THIS DOESN'T LOOK LIKE GARBAGE BURNING. SOMETHING'S WRONG!
IT SMELLS LIKE SMOKE! THE BLAST ALSO SOUNDED VERY CLOSE. I'M AFRAID THE WAREHOUSE IS GOING TO GO UP IN FIRE! HELP! I'D BETTER GET OUT OF HERE SOMEHOW!
HASHEM, PLEASE HELP ME! I HAVE NO IDEA HOW TO GET OUT OF HERE!
I'LL TRY BREAKING THE WINDOW AGAIN WITH TATTE'S LOOP PART.
BOOM! BOOM!

BOOM! BOOM!

WALLA, WHAT WAS THAT?! WHAT'S HAPPENING INSIDE ABDUL'S HOUSE?

BRING SOME WATER QUICK! WATER! BEFORE THE ENTIRE VILLAGE GOES UP IN FLAMES!

IT'S A FIRE! SOMEONE CALL THE FIREFIGHTERS!

I'M RUNNING TO GET THE FIREFIGHTERS. DOUSE THE FIRE WITH WATER! AND SAND TOO!

HELP! HELP!! IFZAHULI! IFZAHULI*!!!

WHAT HAPPENED? WHERE?

MAHMOUD, WHAT HAPPENED TO YOU?!

WHERE'S YOUR FATHER?

ABU AND HALIL HAVE BEEN INJURED IN THE BLAST! CALL AN AMBULANCE!

HALIL WAS PLAYING AROUND WITH ABU'S GRENADE...

GRENADE?! WHAT WAS HE DOING WITH A GRENADE?!

THANK YOU, HASHEM! THIS IS JUST ABOUT ENOUGH FOR ME TO CLIMB OUT...

I'M FINALLY FREE! I'M JUST FEELING A BIT DIZZY, AND MY LEGS ARE SHAKY... BUT I CAN'T WAIT EVEN A SECOND. EVERYONE MUST BE SO WORRIED ABOUT ME.

* HELP!

LOOK OVER THERE! ONE OF THE HOUSES IS BURNING. THEY'RE ALL BUSY TRYING TO PUT IT OUT.
WHO'S GOING TO HELP US SEARCH FOR BARUCHKE? THEY'RE ALL BUSY WITH THE FIRE.
WE NEED TO FIND YUSUF.
YUSUF'S BOOTH IS CLOSED. I GUESS HE'S OUT HELPING PUT OUT THE FIRE.
I KNOW FIRST AID. LET'S GO. I'LL OFFER MY HELP, AND MAYBE WE'LL LEARN SOME HELPFUL INFORMATION.
HEY, I'M A PARAMEDIC. WHO NEEDS HELP?
HERE, COME HERE! ABDUL AND HIS SON SEEM TO BE IN CRITICAL CONDITION!
BRING ME SOME CLEAN SHEETS, WATER, SOAP AND ALCOHOL!
YOU NEED HELP, REB TZVI?
I'LL MANAGE HERE WITH THE ARABS' ASSISTANCE. YOU GO SEARCH FOR BARUCHKE!
I'M COOLING THE BURNS.
OH, HASHEM, PLEASE PROTECT MY PRECIOUS SON, BARUCH *BEN* BAILA, WHEREVER HE IS! PLEASE MAKE SURE NOTHING BAD HAPPENS TO HIM. HELP US BRING HIM HOME SAFE AND SOUND!

BARUCHKE! WHERE WERE YOU?! EVERYONE'S SEARCHING FOR YOU!
IN THE SHUL, WHICH SERVES AS THE *CHEDER* CLASSROOM TOO:
WHERE'S TATTE?
HE RODE OVER TO IBN IBRAQ WITH REB TZVI TO LOOK FOR YOU!
OY, YOU'RE VERY PALE, BARUCHKE! MOTTELE, GO GET SOMETHING FOR YOUR BROTHER TO EAT.
WE'RE SO HAPPY TO SEE YOU, BARUCHKE! WE WERE SO WORRIED ABOUT YOU! DON'T WORRY, MOTTELE. WE'LL SEND SOMEONE QUICKLY TO TELL YOUR FATHER THAT YOU'RE BACK.
TELL HIM THAT ALL THE STOLEN MERCHANDISE IS INSIDE ABDUL'S WAREHOUSE!
REALLY?! AND WHERE HAVE YOU BEEN?!
ABDUL LOCKED ME UP IN THAT SAME WAREHOUSE!
OY, VEY! WHAT A MIRACLE THAT YOU MANAGED TO ESCAPE!
YOSSELE WAS RIGHT, THEN.
THERE'S A LOT GOING ON IN IBN IBRAQ NOW. A BLAST, AND FIRE, AND...
I'LL ASK REB YISRAEL TO HEAD OVER THERE WITH THE HORSE AND WAGON SO THAT HE CAN BRING THE MERCHANDISE BACK. HE'LL INFORM REB ITCHE AND REB TZVI THAT THE BOY'S BACK, AND HELP THEM CARRY ALL THE FABRICS BACK TO THE BNEI BRAK. LET'S DAVEN THAT THEY MAKE IT BACK QUICKLY!

THOSE FIREFIGHTERS! BY THE TIME THEY CAME, THERE WAS NOTHING LEFT TO SAVE OF ABDUL'S HOUSE.
BUT THEY SAVED THE REST OF THE VILLAGE. THEY STOPPED THE FIRE FROM SPREADING FURTHER.
I CAN'T BELIEVE HOW KIND THOSE YAHUD ARE. RABBI SVI SAVED POOR HALIL'S LIFE. DID YOU SEE HOW HE DID CPR ON HIM?
SURE I SAW. HE TREATED ABDUL TOO. IF NOT FOR HIM, ABDUL WOULD HAVE BEEN DEAD BY THE TIME THE AMBULANCE ARRIVED.
AND LOOK AT THOSE YAHUD OVER THERE! THEY'RE EMPTYING OUT ABDUL'S WAREHOUSE TO SAVE HIS POSSESSIONS FROM THE FIRE!
I WONDER WHERE ABDUL GOT ALL THOSE ROLLS OF FABRIC FROM. I DIDN'T KNOW HE STARTED A NEW BUSINESS IN ADDITION TO SELLING WATERMELONS!
THERE, REB ITCHE. YOUR FABRICS ARE ALL LOADED.
THANK YOU, REB YISRAEL. LET'S HEAD BACK TO BNEI BRAK NOW. I MUST SEE MY SON, BARUCHKE!
OW!! OUCH!!! IT'S ALL BECAUSE OF THOSE YAHUD! THEIR G-D IS PUNISHING ME FOR STEALING FROM THEM!
IN BNEI BRAK:
WHAT A HUGE MIRACLE WE HAD, CHILDREN! BARUCHKE IS BACK HERE, SAFE AND SOUND, AND SO ARE REB YISRAELOVICH'S FABRICS. WHAT DO YOU SAY WE HOLD A BIG SEUDAS HODAYAH TO THANK HASHEM FOR HIS GREAT CHASSADIM WITH US?
THE MEN WHO WENT OUT TO THE ARAB VILLAGE SHOULD BE BACK ANY MINUTE NOW. LET'S HEAD OUT TO GREET THEM WITH SONGS AND DANCING!

חַסְדֵי ה' כִּי לֹא תָמְנוּ כִּי לֹא כָלוּ רַחֲמָיו!!!
OOOH, WHAT A WELCOME THE CHILDREN HAVE ARRANGED FOR US!
BARUCHKE! MOTTELE!!
WE EXPERIENCED SUCH EXACT, AMAZING *HASHGACHAH*! SUCH *NISSIM*! BARUCHKE IS BACK, AND EVEN OUR MERCHANDISE HAS BEEN FOUND. NOW I'LL BE ABLE TO REOPEN THE BUSINESS, AND WITH HASHEM'S HELP, BRING MAMA AND THE BABY TO US!
SEE? ALL'S WELL THAT ENDS WELL! MOST IMPORTANTLY, WE'RE BACK TO BEING CLOSE BROTHERS. I THINK WE BOTH REALIZED JUST HOW MUCH WE APPRECIATE AND LOVE EACH OTHER. LET'S NEVER, EVER FIGHT AGAIN!
ONE MONTH LATER:
MOTTELE AND BARUCHKE, WE'RE GOING TO THE PORT NOW TO WAIT FOR THE BOAT THAT'S BRINGING MAMA AND THE BABY!
I CAN SEE THE SHORES OF ERETZ YISRAEL, WHERE MY HUSBAND AND CHILDREN MUST BE WAITING FOR ME. OH, I MISS MY FAMILY SO MUCH!
MOTTELE! LOOK! THERE'S THE BOAT!
MAMA! MAMA!
THE END

Many years have passed since the twins' story took place. They are grandfathers by now! We asked them to respond to a few questions. Here is what they had to say:

Howls in the Dunes is a fictional story, which means that it never actually happened, but the background is based on true facts. Yes, this is how Bnei Brak was built by a handful of *frum* families. The historical facts were taken from books that researched this topic.*

The city of Bnei Brak received its name from its location. It was built on the very lands where the ancient city of Bnei Brak, which we read about in *Sefer Yehoshua*, in the Haggadah, and in other sources, once stood. Bnei Brak was initially built near the Arab village Ibn Ibraq, which is also named after the biblical city of Bnei Brak.

The Arab village existed until 5708, but was renamed even earlier to El-Chiriyah. The remnants of the village remain until today in the Chiriyah garbage disposal site near Mesubim – a city named so because of the *Rabbanim* mentioned in the Haggadah who were "*Mesubim*" in Bnei Brak. Givat Shmuel nearby was built over the ruins of Ibn Ibraq.

The visionary behind the building of Bnei Brak was Rav Yitzchak Gershtenkorn, z"l.

Rabbi Gershtenkorn served as the emissary for Yidden from Warsaw who wanted to settle Eretz Yisrael and build a city that will follow the Torah and Mitzvos. They received an approval and *brachos* from the *Gedolei Hador* of that generation, such as the Gerrer Rebbe zt"l, the Alexander Rebbe zt"l, the Rebbe of Radzimin zt"l, and more.

The story of Yossele, who fell from the automobile while playing with his friends, is also a true story, with some minor changes to the details. The child recovered from his wounds after enduring a long period of suffering.

Bnei Brak today is a city filled with tall buildings and many, many shuls and *yeshivos*. One of them must have been built by our fictional character, Mottele! Do you think so, too?

The purchase contract with the Arab land-owners was signed in 5682.

The reason the settlers chose to build a city in the center of the country and not live in Yerushalayim, for example, was because they were looking for a place that will provide them with a source of livelihood as well. Bnei Brak was close to Tel Aviv, a port city, which offered more *parnassah* opportunities.

Bnei Brak had the great *zechus* of being home to some of our greatest *gedolim*. Two, for example, were **Rav Avraham Yeshayah Karelitz – the Chazon Ish** zt"l, who shaped the city's spiritual character for more than two decades until his passing, and **Rav Chaim Kanievsky** zt"l.

* *Al Chomotayich Bnei Brak* by Rabbi Yitzchak Meir, z"l, and *Chevlei Yotzer* by, yblc"t, Rabbi Aharon Sorasky, shli"ta.

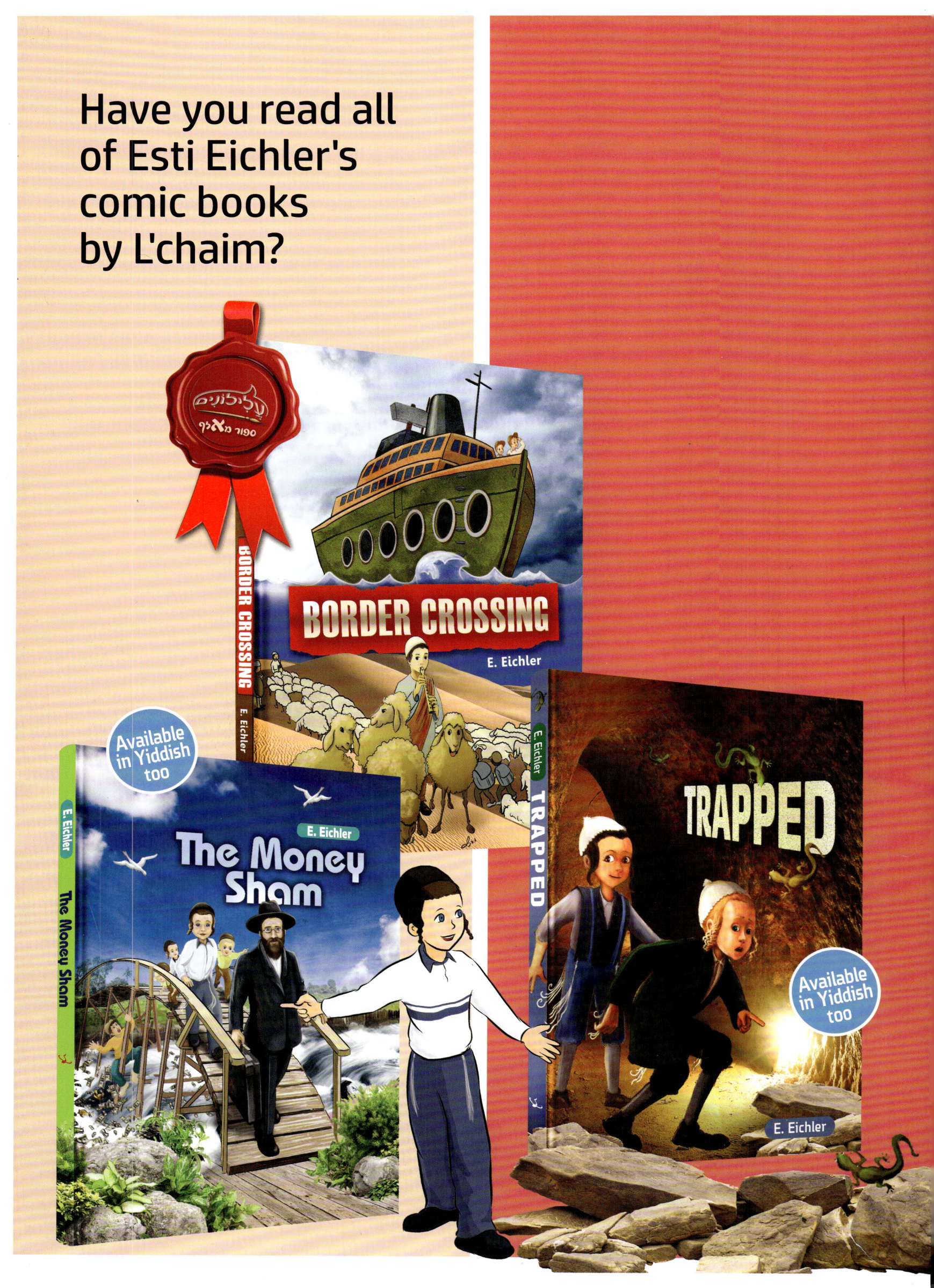

Have you read all of Esti Eichler's comic books by L'chaim?

BORDER CROSSING — E. Eichler

The Money Sham — E. Eichler
Available in Yiddish too

TRAPPED — E. Eichler
Available in Yiddish too